Short Poems to Memorize

By David E. Lay

Charles West Cope, artist

Author Bio: David E. Lay is a retired teacher, finally realizing his lifelong dream of writing prose and poetry. His mother was a writer, poet, and a librarian, and this, he believes, is where his original inspiration came from. His very first attempt at writing was a thirty-three-page-long original motion picture script, typed on his father's 1911 Underwood typewriter, when he was fourteen years old.

Copyright ©2023 by David E Lay

All rights reserved, including the right of reproduction in whole or in part in any form.

ISBN: 979-8-9895327-1-1

33 32 31 30 29 28 27 26 25 24 23   1 2 3 4 5 6 7 8 9 10

Printed in the   United States

Cover Design Credit: David E. Lay
Gabriel Joseph Marie Augustin Ferrier, artist 1880

Images used in this book are either public domain, photos by, or AI generated images based on descriptions by David E. Lay. AI platforms used: Perchance.org, ArtGuru.ai, Adobe Firefly. Attempts to give proper credit to artists are based on searches through Google Images, https://images.google.com/

"Were dreams my ultimate end,
And reality lay there, too,
Then my place here is naught
But the experience of imaginings..."
D.E. Lay

Contents

How to read my poetry 1

So, here it begins… 3

Valentine's Day 5

Happiness in Our Thoughts 7

Cupid's Arrow 9

Would You Be My Friend? 11

Sit With Me 13

New Birth 15

Stirrings 17

Speak to the Morning Sun 19

Those Places We Do Not See 21

The Awkwardness of Spring 23

Mother Lingers There 25

Mother's Hand 27

Wynds 29

The Road to That Place So High 31

The Bidding of Spring 33

The Cradle 35

Ancestor's Place 37

Footsteps 39

Memorial Day 41

Songs of Children 43

Sleep 45

Morning's Touch 47

Heaven on Earth 49

The Breath of Summer	51
Oh, Summer	53
Remembrance of a Dinner Table	55
The Odor of Soft	57
9/11	59
Loved, Simply	61
A Gathering of Souls	63
Make Thy Coffin, Friend	65
Practicing What's Yet to Come	67
Future's Call	69
The Fabric of Our Being	71
The Kitten	73
Smells of Mist	75
A Penny in My Shoe	77
Heart's Dance	79
The East Wynd	81
Plenty on My Plate	83
Moonlight Walk	85
Soft Verdure	87
Sleeping Songs Yet Sung	89
Gentle Souls	91
Geese in Migration	93
What Earth Gives You	95
O' Mousy	97
Harvest Moon	99
Break Thy Bread	101

Is This Morning New?	103
Thoughts of Souls Now Gone	105
Seeking Truths	107
Take Heed	109
Tome of Old	111
Giving Alms	113
Dreams Read by Candlelight	115
Grief	117
Were I a Cloud	119
On the Pond at Night	121
Heart's Intent	123
Through the Old Window	125
Quiet Hours of Thought	127
The Early Sun	129
October Night	131
Where Amathyst Gleams	133
That Place You Imagine	135
Come Night, Leave Not a Trace	137
Morning Light	139
Spirits of Night	141
Gespenst (Ghosts)	143
Lil' Boy this Morning	145
Ode to a Tree Stump	147
Points in Space	149
I Gather Upon My Shoes	151
If There Be Gods	153

Prepare This Day	155
Job is Done	157
The Beginning of Tomorrow	159
Angels Sense Our Steps	161
Entanglement	163
A Simple Moment	165
The First Spark	167
Exhilaration	169
Winter's Solstice	171
Where is That Moment?	173
Where Small Creatures Sleep	175
Snowflakes	177
Life, Itself, Its Own Reason	179
Peace on Earth	181
Christmas Eve	183
Good Christmas Morn	185
Where Flows This Day?	187
Winter Moon	189
The Depth of a Soul	191
Give No More Than Morning is Able	193
What Stirs Here Below?	195
My Place Here is Naught	197
Return Of The Rooks	199
The Long Sleep	201
Give Me No End, Friend	203

How to read my poetry

When I write poetry, it is usually by looking at a picture and the first line of the poem comes to me in a simple thought, but then I always ask myself how can I say this without really saying it? That is where the work begins, and the creative muse laughs at me for the struggle, but ultimately the work wins over the muse.

The poems in this book were written over time, and my earlier poems were usually written in simple four lines where the second and forth lines rhymed; sometimes, though, I would write in short prose poetry, often with as few as three lines where nothing rhymed, but it had a "poetic" feel to it. These are the easiest to read out loud, and perhaps to memorize.

As I wrote more, I developed a bit more sophisticated style where I started writing five-line poems: The first line rhymes with the last line and the middle three lines are descriptive, giving hints of the meaning of the poem. In essence, these poems are poems within poems, with the middle three lines usually, though not always, rhyming. These are the most difficult to read and memorize but carry with them much deeper meaning than the other styles.

Last, I have included passages from some of my short stories and novel that are prose, but, again, have a poetic feel to them. Probably easier to read than the five-line style, but more difficult to find the not-so-apparent rhythm of the poem.

So, here it begins…

My poetry, roughly laid out in order of season, shared with you for your pleasure, and, hopefully, some enlightenment…

Charles West Cope, artist, "Devotion"

Valentine's Day

There once was a day,
I can't remember its name,
Where one would say "I love you",
And the other would say "the same".

William Holman Hunt, artist,

Happiness in Our Thoughts

In my contemplations, I have determined, over time,
That there's more to this reality than meets the eye,
And that happiness in our thoughts
Become as prayers, attracting angels from on high,
Who listen intently and measure our words for rhyme.

Gabriel Joseph Marie Augustin Ferrier, artist 1880

Cupid's Arrow

Can you give me any other reason to say
"I love you" without knowing it's so,
With your heart a target supple,
If friend Cupid has strung his keen bow,
And his arrow has pierced your breast today?

William Bouguereau, artist

Would You Be My Friend?

Would you be my friend if I sit next to you?
Can you tell me secrets that you know?
Do you like the sunshine?
Can you smell the rain, and feel the snow?
It seems to me your cheeks with red imbue!

D.E. Lay, digital image

Sit With Me

"Sit with me for a while and speak of things to come",

"No, not yet, this moment still warms my heart",

Said I,

"I wish not to yield to time, to pull this moment apart",

"Oh", said they, "then I shall leave and wait for you at home."

Seignac Guillaume, artist, Psyche

New Birth

Winds glance and caress Earth's heights above,
Stirred with sparks in Sky's curtains seen,
Born of the Sun,
There Great chariots deliver new wonder keen,
Like Angels gently pulling her with radiant love.

D.E. Lay, digital image

Stirrings

Seeds of cold fell delicate leaves from above,
Falling to white clad smothered heath,
Spawning hope of that to come,
When jonquils anxious stirs beneath,
And promise of a warming glow of love.

Joseph Farquharson, artist, 1903

Speak to the Morning Sun

Speak to the morning Sun, speak to the dew,
Speak of winds calmed from trees bent,
Tell of the night's cold,
Tell of North's bitter breath hard sent,
And sigh, bathing now in their sweet warming hue.

D. E. Lay, digital image

Those Places We Do Not See

Beneath it all, in those places we do not see,
Under branch and blade and nettles,
Deep within our sightless eye,
There are those beings who are ancient,
Who, by gods, are themselves forever to be.

Florence Vernon, artist

The Awkwardness of Spring

Is there anyone more awkward than Spring?
She is angry, then sad, then happy, then mad,
And yet I can think of no one I'd rather be with,
...This time of year...
Oh, and she brings with her friends, some who
twitter and sing!

D.E. Lay, digital image

Mother Lingers There

Haloed by window's misted sky's estuary,
Hidden in memory's box, mother lingers still,
Scented by sweet garden's patina,
Wafts yearning to hear songs of Singer's drill,
Weaving long threads into satin vestiary.

Vincent Romero, artist

Mother's Hand

Were I to walk with you again,
Would you hold my hand?
Would you paint for me those scenes?
You remember, those times before me,
and create in me new dreams?

Hans Andersen Brendekildt, artist

Wynds

(I like to mimic some of my favorite poets. Here I try to mimic Robert Burns)

A wind is buildin' o'er heaths,
moors 'n glen,
Liftin' the weigh' of oceans to sky,
'N me, here, jus' watchin'
The tossels of cholum 'n birds flitter'n by,
'N thunder yon tellin' o' gods' disfavor of men.

Rodolphe Bresdin, artist. Trees Bending in the Wind

The Road to That Place So High
To Michael D.

Pray the road to that place so high, so steep,
Where Angels lift souls above,
Gives no encumbrance
To winged arms which hold in love,
And give him gently over, dear soul to keep.
Pax requiem, Tonito

B. Plockhurst, artist

The Bidding of Spring

Though Spring has no say in what is to come,
But in stormy fights to push back North,
And she sings morning songs,
Encouraging buds and nests come forth,
While she dresses the entrance for Sol to enter from.

D.E. Lay, digital image

The Cradle

Did the mountains send us gentle rivers cold,
So valleys could cradle our den
In beds of cool grasses,
And send gentle breaths over that fen,
There standing over us, like guardians of old?

Albert Bierstadt, artis, Storm 1870

Ancestor's Place

Step into dreams of ancestor's ancient place,
Lingering among long gone labors there,
Torn by time's brutal hammer,
Given to Mother's incessant song bare,
Befriending fading whisperer's quiet space.

D.E. Lay, digital image

Footsteps

Had voice outside pierced air and glass
Had footsteps befell the garden path,
And soft breath 'Hellooo' resounded,
Then thunder booms were dreams,
And smiles would cause worries pass.

Robert Morley, artist, 1918, He Awaits His Master's Return from War

Memorial Day

The things they carried, they carried lite,
Things remembered of love and home,
A youth's heart of endless sight,
Of unlived adventures there in future's roam,
In their hearts, they carried youth's hope bright.

US Soldier carrying Vietnamese child,
Photographer not attributed.

Songs of Children

Distant thunders tell a future to come,
Give no heed to troubles now,
Sit here cradled to breast,
Sheltered in love's sacred vow,
And listen to songs children once sung.

Charles West, artist. "Reading

Sleep

Sleep, then, and take your soul to dreams afar,
Floating into sweet zephyr puffs,
Tasting clouds' unwept rains,
Seeing, there, below, rising white tufts,
And you lifting, spreading, gossamer laminar!"

D.E. Lay, digital image

Morning's Touch

Are there still touches, light and whisp,
Upon the head, like the sweet
Memory of mother's breath,
When waking in the Earthly turn,
And sleep gives way to morning crisp?

D.E. Lay, digital image

Heaven on Earth

If instead of wishing for wings to fly,
Where only above my realm was sky,
But were I to use mine that's given,
To feel the sweet Earth beneath...
That's Heaven!

D.E. Lay, digital image

The Breath of Summer

Were my Summers filled with soft blown curtains and friends,
I would think there would be no other life as delicious
As smells of earth
Wafting in and out as breathing moments auspicious,
And I holding simple words and thoughts until infinity ends.

D.E. Lay, digital image

Oh, Summer

Oh, Summer, yield soon unto us thy breast of plenty,
Seed to bread flour is yet by mill's turn made,
While corn livens in bright day's oven,
And gentle beings seek succor in lone tree's shade;
Give unto us that from which Sun spills in weeks twenty.

Willem Meris, artist

Remembrance of a Dinner Table

Sometimes light, placed just so, gives to me a smell,
And there mother clinks fork to plate, smiles, sighs,
Brothers smother laughs,
Father with mischief in mouth and eyes,
And takes me to a time of laughter and stories to tell.

Bertha Wegmann, artist, 1891

The Odor of Soft

Is softness as strong a feel as smell, I ask,
For the comfort of soft has an odor,
That which brings to my arms
A memory of longing, of a rising tide,
To protect, yet drawn to its light to bask.

Emil Osterman, artist, 1910

9/11

Stay, while whet upon edge sounding rings,
Look, there is task enough here,
Where hand in hand they fall,
While breath is held from dust filled fear,
And, oh, friend scythe, how agony in chorus
sings

D.E. Lay, digital image

Loved, Simply

Find in me that child who was once loved simply, completely,
For no other reason than my existence;
Not from demands of faith,
Nor from avaricious insistence,
But from a heart grown warm from my smile given sweetly

John Calcott Horsley, artist

A Gathering of Souls

Should there be a gathering of souls in distant mists,
I would mourn their leaving as Sun lifts them up,
Carrying them to heavens beyond,
Taken from me and my joy of their presence sup,
And I, now alone, feel Sun's calling in that warm light kissed.

Photo by D E. Lay, Morning mist on the South Farm

Make Thy Coffin, Friend

Should the woodsman ask the tree,
What should I make of such grandeur?
Yet would that giant speak, slowly,
In words only his kin could hear,
Make thy coffin, friend, for you are me.

D.E. Lay, digital image

Practicing What's Yet to Come

Give me moments of children's play,
Practicing what's yet to come,
Where I find those times when learning pleased,
And times where imagined work was done.

Paul Herman Wagner, artist

Future's Call

What steps do we take to lift ourselves to higher ground,
Though we can still taste the smell of home,
Drawn to morning routines of old,
Giving us pause, tempting us not to roam,
But the call is strong, seeking what new thoughts can be found?

Norman Rockwell, artist

The Fabric of Our Being

Is the fabric of our being woven with loving care,
With yarn made from star's inner kiln,
Tempered with dark sky's rue,
Treadled by angel's rhythmic spinning milln,
Or is it the makings of Ebils, twining djinn's hair?

Artist unknown, Dutch or French, c~1885, black chalk on paper.
Thought to be a Leon Augustin Lhermitte, or possibly an Anton
Mauve. VanGogh often copied works by Lhermitte.

The Kitten

(From my short story "The Kitten")

A tiny claw holds to roughened skin and sparks a thought
Which erupts a pang, at that little point in all our hearts
Where heaven placed sadness,
And like a sore it spreads, heavy, like a weight, pushing against breastbone,
Wanting to explode to a heave, a sigh.
She closes her eyes and feels again tiny fingers on younger skin, a time long past.

Andrew Wyeth, artist

Smells of Mist

I see in that coral labyrinth a lost place I once played,
Deep in my mind's eye where smells of mist Dampened my face,
And tree's light flickered on auburn hair kissed,
There, too, where friends by me in quiet awe staid.

Maxfield Parrish, artist, The Old Glen Mill, 1950

A Penny in My Shoe

There felt in my shoe
An irritant, a stone or pebble, perhaps.
Then, sitting on a rock, shaking
That trodden pediment,
There fell upon the road a penny,
Small, but mighty, too!

D.E. Lay, digital image

Heart's Dance

Do not pass him who asks with begging eyes,
He, who only asks for your simple glance,
Whose ghost sits behind watching,
Wants only a voice touching heart's dance,
Give him, then, your presence, hear his silent cries.

D.E. Lay, photo of Lil Boy in the East field

The East Wynd

Happy are those who follow clouds above,
They, seeking the East wynd's silent song,
Flying with calm mettle,
As angels spreading shadows long,
For they will find the dove's branch of love

John Bauer, artist

Plenty on My Plate

I see you have enough, my friend,
But here, I have more.
Though my cup is full,
and on my plate there's plenty,
There is always room for friendship,
and with you I share what I adore.

D.E. Lay, Digital Image in the style of John Constable

Moonlight Walk

Continue this given day into night with measured pace,
Sip still air through lips in meters of hope,
Tasting its sweetened breath,
Hearing the old tale of Earth's ancient trope,
Seeking each step to find there a greater grace.

D.E. Lay, Digital Image

Soft Verdure

Given once to peace, taken in morsels to dine,
Gently laid out in splendor there,
On tables of soft verdure,
And with souls of kindred ilk to bare,
We yearn, then, to taste its sweet nectar fine.

D.E. Lay, Digital Image

Sleeping Songs Yet Sung

Find depth in that which seems quieted, still,
Deep below are sleeping songs yet sung,
Sounds made in ethereal dales,
Psalms into blue skies like arrows flung,
For there lay wonders of dreams to fulfill.

Gerard Dou, artist

Gentle Souls

There above, gentle souls, flirtatious, raise,
Groundlings cease for moments of stay,
Following movement aloft,
Gifted visions of sweet gentle play,
And eyes, seeing their fluttering, lift in praise.

Arthur Heyer, artist

Geese in Migration

Go they there, lifting, keeping small distance apart,
Sensing the harsh breath of Norse winds,
Passing in peace,
Each to other in claxon voice 'Follow!' sends,
Leaving us below yearning, touching only our heart.

N.C. Wyeth, artist

What Earth Gives You

Take what good Earth gives you and give her loving tribute,
Giving chilled breathed songs while harvest's gleaned,
Sing to her your praises of thanks,
And laying of hands upon sore torn fields weaned,
As she folds, sleeping, into the blanket of winter's repute.

N.C.Wyeth, artist

O' Mousy

(In some of my poems, I try to imitate some of my favorite poets. This one is similar to the Robert Burn's poem "To a Mouse")

Atop o' that, mousey yon on pumpkin bare,
See 'm? He eats his berries one by one,
But keeps a watchful eye
For those with mal intent, poised,
Feet ready to spring; yes there, right there!

D.E. Lay, Digital Image created in Adobe Firefly

Harvest Moon

What light here touches Earth's semblance and shadows loom,
Where cats hunt as souls sigh in peace recline,
Dreams bathing in feigned warmth,
Feet treading in leaf strewn floor laid out supine,
And eyes see love's trace while hidden Sun kisses yon Moon.

Ivan Aivazovsky, artist, 1879

Break Thy Bread

Is this not our day to fulfill that promise of old?
Do we not have enough to serve the ill?
Are we so poor as to not
Share even a crumb from fortune's mill?
Come, then, break thy bread in true valor bold.

John Henry Witt, artist

Is This Morning New?

Is this morning new, sunlight flotsam on mist?
In it secret patterns in paths it slowly shows,
From here to yon, I see that now,
Giving me a wink, flashed rays on leafy glows,
Yes, it is new, and I glean a smile from its gist.

D.E. Lay photo, "Morning mist"

Thoughts of Souls Now Gone

Give to them the thoughts of souls now gone,
Take not from them their time of play,
But sing to them stories of whim,
And draw lines of reflection that weave a day,
Finding in that labyrinth births of idea's song.

Briton Riviere, artist

Seeking Truths

Understand that which appears complexing,
Seek truths in that which lies beneath,
Touch the simplicity,
But glean from it what the spirits bequeath,
Therein find paths through forests perplexing.

Sarah Paxton Ball Dodson, artist

Take Heed

Take heed, you, of sounds unlikely made
By friend or kin, beware of derision.
Let not voices falsely raised
Turn our heads to make division;
Stay, rather, the course paters painfully laid.

Louis Emile Villa, artist

Tome of Old

The story told that day which held tome of old,
Buried thoughts brought from depth,
A string of life before now,
Weaving histories of ancient breadth,
Words from aged lips once uttered bold.

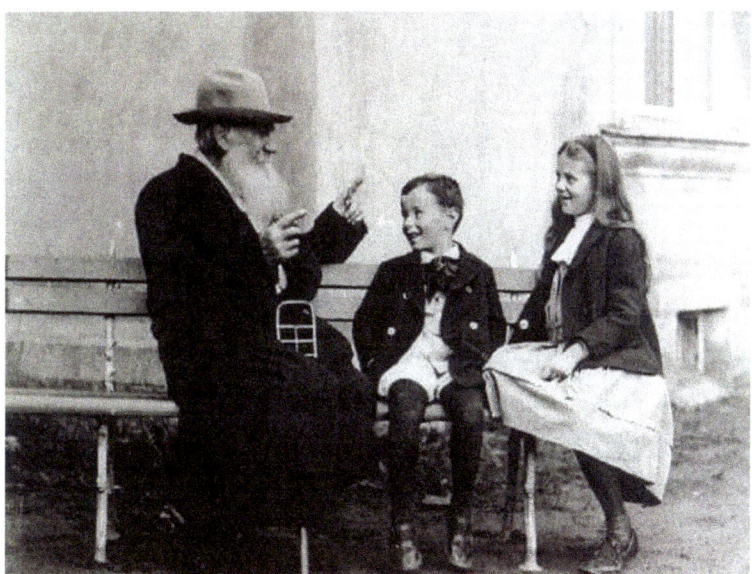

Leo Tolstoy, telling a story to his grandchildren, 1909

Giving Alms

Give not coin or dollar, nor give advice,
Nor place blame for losing hope;
Give alms, instead, of silence,
Of time as a friend, a bulwark to cope,
And allow no sound where a gentle touch will suffice.

A.I. Digital Image, in the Pre-Raphaelite style

Dreams Read by Candlelight

What tale here is told in the quiet of night,
When dreams are read by candle's light,
And listening ears perked toward
Small lips speaking of giant's plight,
Soft voice low, but whispers stir mind's sight?

D.E. Lay, Digital Image

Grief

Who but that old miser, Grief, left to his ways,
Could build a torn heart from sweet home,
Clenching the depth of our being,
Letting us not to step away from gloom,
And he burrows into that little place and stays.

Antonio Rotta, artist

Were I a Cloud

Were I a cloud over this, my path I hold,
I would see long trod travels ahead,
Many paths to choose,
But the way I go I must hold my stead,
And looking behind I see thorns of gold.

D.E. Lay photo, "Distance"

On the Pond at Night

Geese stir the silent night on the pond below,
Songs sung with ancient voices in flight
A thousand years calling Sun,
But dreams, reluctant, say "stay night,
Keep day at pond's edge, let mind's light glow.

Andrew Wyeth, artist

Heart's Intent

Bell towers, arches, made in elegant spires,
In some likeness of heart's intent,
Stone on stone carved well,
Seen with head turned and neck bent,
Yet, life's thromb is here, deep in breast's fires.

Luc Oliveir-Merson, artist

Through the Old Window
(From my novel, "The Man Who Watched A Pig Sleeping")

"Through that old window he saw a murderous
cacophony of black spirits,
Holding a congress of some great meaning,
Angered by a chattering red visitant
Who raised the question of propriety."

D.E. Lay, Digital Image

Quiet Hours of Thought

Walk gently in those quite hours of thought,
When morning sings in tones of light,
Spinning ray's thread,
Weaving mist's blanket glimmering bright,
'n embrace this moment from eternity bought.

D.E. Lay photo, "Suessy in the morning mist"

The Early Sun

Who calls the early sun, evoking spirit rays,
Seeking warm respite from night's chill,
Storm's brief insult no better,
Affecting breath's stutter, lung's fettle ill,
Bawl, then, and beckon 'til warmth with us stays.

D.E. Lay photo, "Peaches and calf"

October Night

Tree gyrates in rhythms born of bluster,
Rapping hard against roof 'n' sill,
Ne'er ignoring her call,
She who lived here once, but still
Calling for you to play, with joy's lost fluster.

Portrait of a girl unknown, 1860's

Where Amathyst Gleams

Tell me again of where amathyst gleams,
Where light sparkles dew clothed trees,
Where spirits give salve
To saddened hearts lifted by phaeries,
And tell me again of beauty in sweet little things.

Gustave Dore, artist

That Place You Imagine

In this portal to that place you imagine,
Where the soul gives a soft sigh,
Where there is no evil,
Where the gentle Mother lay bye,
Is it there life seeks healing amandine?

D.E. Digital Image

Come Night, Leave Not a Trace

Come night, leave not a trace here,
This place needs what Sun gives,
And slip into the shadows,
Peeking once to see what life lives,
Return again when Moon seeks skies clear.

D.E. Lay, Digital Image

Morning Light

Look, then, to the morning light, friend,
Gradually filling, a stoup pouring gold,
Shadows meld with detail,
Giving to blue blandness colors bold,
Drawing lines, bringing night's shadows end.

Andrew Wyeth, artist

Spirits of Night

Er the spirits of night be caught sleeping,
They lift in quiet mass from dale below,
Each with careful step,
Discreetly, not to wake fawn or doe,
Then rising into heaven's hands safe keeping.

D.E. Lay photo, "Mist off Beaver Creek"

Gespenst (Ghosts)
(From my short story, "Gespenst")

"Are there ghosts?" she asked.
"Yes, I imagine there are ghosts", her mother said.
"But isn't that the point? Imagining, I mean".
Her mother paused, raising her head, looked out the window,
Seeing what light cannot bask…

Andrew Wyeth, artist

Lil' Boy this Morning

He laid in rest, my behemoth, this morning,
Each breath a billowing cloud,
In peaceful vigilance over the South Field,
Where foe dare not enter... A warning!

D.E. Lay photo, "Lil Boy resting in the South pasture"

Ode to a Tree Stump

In my heart I find you, like your quite sound,
A multitude of hands waving to the sky,
Pushed by gentle winds,
Like a thousand songs, sung at once,
Lost in sight, yet in hearing you are found.

D.E. Lay, Digital Image

Points in Space

From small lights come points in space
To give seeking eyes solace,
And solace is found
In axis converged for each its own,
Where they call home, and home its place.

D.E. Lay, Digital Image

I Gather Upon My Shoes

I gather upon my shoes the dust of gladness,
The smell of winter bites sweetly my nose,
The spring of my step lifts me,
The cold fresh breeze blusters my face,
And hither to yon alieves all past sadness.

Norman Rockwell, artist

If There Be Gods

If there be gods nearby, in woods and fields,
In misty light upon our backs,
Then grant us peace, and,
Thee, who live in hidden time and space,
Give us solace in grasses and tangled shields.

D.E. Lay photo, "Autumn, North pasture on the South Farm"

Prepare This Day

Prepare this day with mist and subtle light,
Take up no plow nor scythe in hand,
Give rue no special quarter,
But break the cold air before you
With mouthed awe at such privileged sight.

D.E. Lay, Digital image

Job is Done

When the job is done and rest is needed,
Do not lay in the bed of laurels,
Nor let ear bend to praise,
But linger there in that place
Where friends gather, and joy is heeded.

D.E. Lay, Digital Image

The Beginning of Tomorrow

Haggard, thy mid-week to darn beginning to end,
Like a celestial tik and tacking,
The knitting of what has been
To the beginning of tomorrow, and next,
On to weave Saturn's Day, a renewal to send.

Peter Vilhelm Ilsted, artist

Angels Sense Our Steps

Who but angels can sense our next step,
Where toe follows heal,
And eyes gaze hollow,
Yet for her quiet singing peal,
Our path winds are stayed, our will adept.

Fridolin Leiber, artist

Entanglement

All we here, on Earth this night,
Sitting near others,
Or standing far,
If even for a moment, together,
Feel the pull of light orbs bright.

A.I. Digital Image

A Simple Moment

Oh, simple moment of thoughts gone wry,
When I lift my pen to scribe to thee,
Merry This and Happy That,
There pokes above the kind intent
A memory of friends, and sweet time gone by.

Mary Pickford at her desk. Fred Hartsook, photographer, 1918

The First Spark

What sparks that first memory, from when I first recall,
That moment when I sensed excitement,
Setting heart to race and eyes to swell,
And wonder begins its journey to deep mind's becall?

D.E. Lay, Digital Image

Exhilaration

A moment of wind-swept exhilaration tasted,
Every follicle titillated head to toe,
Eyes squinted to waterery,
Stomach pitted at peak and low,
Let life return me to then when youth is wasted.

D.E. Lay, Digital Image

Winter's Solstice
(From my novel "The Man Who Watched a Pig Sleeping")

In darkness light is far reaching,
And even only a small light
Touches the hearts of those so distant.

Emily Gertrude Thompson, artist

Where is That Moment?
(From my short story "The Kitten")

Where is that moment, that second, that sting
That hurls the head-kissed child into adulthood,
Leaving behind an emptying hope for a biding return,
Half hidden by the time worn door,
With following eyes and a mere, stolen, glimpse
Of that untold happy future?

D.E. Lay, Digital Image

Where Small Creatures Sleep

There, where small creatures sleep,
Above their nested beds
Cold beauty sits,
And shadows breath carefully
In awe of what tendrilled prisms keep.

D.E. Lay, Digital Image

Snowflakes

Pause, you, and think of those small lights,
Falling in numbers many, one on one,
Piled delicately each on the other,
Quieting woods and hollow and run,
Giving no sway to echo and wonders benights.

Snowfall, National Park Service image, public domain

Life, Itself, Its Own Reason

Were there to be a life with no cause,
No reason to live other than life itself,
Its own reason,
From passing from womb to strife,
Would it be less if you gave breath pause?

William Adolphe Bouguereau, artist

Peace on Earth

Only can there be peace if it resounds in every heart,
Yet hearts beat out of step with drums of hope,
And callous eyes seek threads to pull,
Weaving from that their songs of selfish trope,
For lyres played untuned gives dissonance its start.

William Adolphe Bouguereau, artist, 1893

Christmas Eve

With a baby calf tucked neatly under my beard,
And a kitty fast asleep on my belly,
I fall asleep, sleeping soundly, dreaming...
...Of peanut butter and jelly.
Peace to all, and to all a good night!

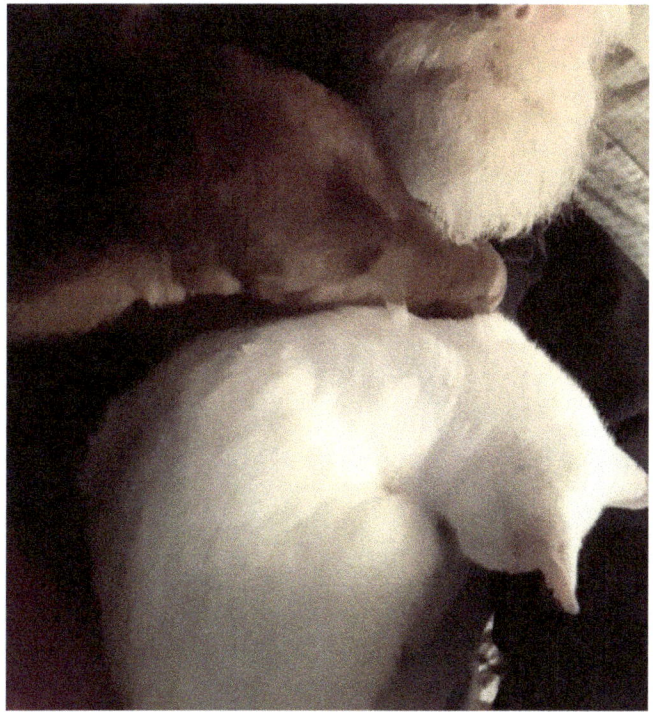

D.E. Lay photo... Selfie with Katrina, the calf born during a snow storm, and Lil Stink, the kitten I raised from a two-day old kitten.

Good Christmas Morn

Carefully, two heads did
rise,
To see golden light just now,
And four peds skipped,
Jumped, and skittered fast,
To see what 'neath the yule tree
lies.

Vintage Christmas Card

Where Flows This Day?
(New Year's Day)

Where flows this day, toward noon or night?
Build we our battlements or our bed?
Lift arm with sword or with flower?
Does not each flow have its ebb?
Choose, child, step you left or step you right?

D.E. Lay photo, "Windbreak"

Winter Moon

Does the winter moon care of its
Aura,
That ring of mystic white glow,
Where chill of night
Seeps to bone, yet here, we, below,
Eyes, bright, seek promise of future
flora?

D.E. Lay, Digital Image

The Depth of a Soul

(From my novel, "The Man Who Watched a Pig Sleeping)

The depth of a soul is excavated
In dollops of misery,
And its strength built, stone by stone,
by the gabion of compassion;
But the bulwark of the soul
Is its opposition to evil.

August Schenk, artist

Give No More Than Morning is Able

Day, give no more than morning is able,
For then Sun's light gives hope anew,
And do not drown that moment,
In minutes lost in toils' aching sinew,
But give promise of a happy evening's table.

Heinrich Gogarten, artist

What Stirs Here Below?

What stirs here below an unsettled milieu,
Not yet yawning from Winter's weep,
Contained in icy tombs
To save for nature's moments keep,
Lifting from petrichor to seek morning's dew?

D.E. Lay, Digital Image

My Place Here is Naught

Were dreams my ultimate end,
And reality lay there, too,
Then my place here is naught
But the experience of imaginings.

Andrew Wyeth, artist

Return Of The Rooks
(Winter's End)

Fluttering's stir where I cannot climb,
And there ebullience is shared amongst that clan,
Though I stand here below, alone,
I am consoled by their return,
As they give measure to end of Winter's span.

Alexei Savrosov, artist... Return of the Rooks

The Long Sleep

Were I asleep, drifting, dreaming of what could be,
Breathing sounds shallow in my chest,
Toks ticking, sparks snaping,
Spirits holding me brow to breast,
Would you reach in that my dream and jostle me?

Britons Riviere, artist, 1868, "The Long Sleep"

Give Me No End, Friend

Give me no end, my friend, to this my story told,
Give me no tombstone, carved in artist's vest,
Under which I might lay alone and cold,
But give me unto that which is nature's best,
Then, please, old friend, share afar my words behold.

The End from public domain images, artist not attributed

www.ingramcontent.com/pod-product-compliance
Lightning Source LLC
Chambersburg PA
CBHW050902160426
43194CB00011B/2256